Janice,
To someone who watched me grow, taught me that in order to succeed you must put God first. You are a great person and I appreciate your life lessons. Thanks for all your support and love.

Shana Jay

A Piece of My Heart

Shana Jay

Copyright © 2010 by Shana Jay

All Rights reserved. No portion of this book may be reproduced in any form without the written permission of the publisher, except in the case of brief quotations in articles or reviews.

Dedication

This book is dedicated to the beholder of the most beautiful brown eyes that do not judge me and accepts me for who I am. You are "The Male Version of Me" I love you more than words can express. Beyond a shadow of a doubt, you are my greatest inspiration.

.

Acknowledgements

I want to acknowledge God because without Him giving me the gift to express my deepest feelings through the art of poetry, this book would not exist. I truly love and adore God for all He is to me, what He has done for me and what He is pruning me to be. I want to thank my mother for introducing me to the idea of putting my thoughts on paper. God brings certain people into our lives for a reason. Jocelynn, I am proud to call you a dear friend, whom I hold close to my heart. Next I want to thank my friend Chasity "the next Tyler Perry in the making". I have always admired you for your dreams and aspirations. I can't wait for us both to make it to the top! Love you!!! How can I forget my semi-circle of friends: Sandra, Kenya, Candace, Natarsha, Tara, Kirsten, Deana, Asha, Shun, Joy and Bridget; without you guys being my support system I honestly don't know how I would have made it through. I can always depend on you all to tell me the truth and I love you for that. Thank you for loving me in a special way. I want to thank my family because no matter what goes on behind closed doors and despite the circumstances, I must say that I can always depend on you. I know my family isn't perfect but without the foundation that has been passed on throughout the years I would not be the woman that I am today. I saved the best for last: Yasmine and Byron Jr. You two are the apple of my eye and I love you dearly. Thank you for loving me unconditionally, flaws and all.

Contents

Chapter 1: My Preferred Heart

Chapter 2: My Affectionate Heart

Chapter 3: My Loathing Heart

Chapter 4: My Sensual Heart

Chapter 5: My Devoted Heart

Chapter 6: My Longing Heart

Chapter 7: My Aching Heart

Chapter 8: My Truth-Seeking Heart

Chapter One:

My Preferred Heart

Lemon Drop Martini

*O*h how I love thee, let me count the ways! When I go to the bar with my girls I can't wait to see you. I daydream about you all day. You make me feel as if I am your one and only but I know better than that. I blush at the thought of how many times you've caused me to be a naughty girl. But who cares, when I am with you, nothing else matters. I look forward to seeing you in your superb splendor. I make sure I look my best for you since we only see each other once a week.

I always want to be at my best when we are near. I wish we could always be together but too much of you is intoxicating! You make it hard for me to hold back at times, but I can't help myself because you make me feel so comfortable. You don't have to ever worry about me being untrue to you even though your actions insist that we have an open relationship. I see how other women stare at you when we are together but I don't get jealous because I know you are mine at that moment.

Nothing else can make me feel the way you do. I love how you allow me to lick the sugar from your strong silhouette. When I taste you, all types of sensations rush through my body. It feels as if you've penetrated me; I almost surrender to the pleasure I feel. My lemon drop martini, you love to tease me and that's cool; I find it enticing. I can't stop coming back for more. Our foreplay cannot be explained, even if I tried.

When it's time to leave, I silently declare my love for you. I think to myself that was so great; I need a smoke because I can hardly walk straight. You always know how to do a girl just right. Until next time, mio dolce amor, a thousand kisses. And although you give me none in return, they still set my soul on fire!

Music

Where would I be without Music for it is my life?

When I hear the rhythm, it makes me feel like I am in heaven. I groove to its different melodies. It doesn't have a color, taste or smell. It has no boundaries.

Music can be sensual, sexy, as well as rough; it can even make you do things that you thought were impossible. Music puts me in a catatonic trance as the lyrics guide my hips while giving me an intense groove. Music is my kryptonite and I am Music's super hero. Sometimes I feel weak while other times I feel strong. But through all these emotions, Music is always there to hold me tight. I love Music because Music loves me.

Music is my support system and that is why I love it so. Music is my therapist, Music is my teacher, Music is my lover and Music is my friend. I am Music's sole survivor. Life would not be the same without it. Music is my all and all, my everything.

The Infamous Color Purple

The infamous color purple is the signature for royalty. I feel like the Queen I was intended to be when I drape myself in the garments shaded with this fascinating color that stands out so boldly. I feel superior to the world, my own super hero at best. When a man steps to me and attempts to feed me those old tired, clichés, I think, you poor, simple-minded fool. How dare you address me in this manner? Do you not realize that you are in the presence of a Queen? Instead, I give him an effortless grin and continue in the manner in which I, royalty, was trained.

I reign in purple. My light shines so bright that not even a dreary, rainy day could dim it. The winds could blow with all their magnitude and force. The rain could flood and make an immense sea but it wouldn't cause my illustrious shade of purple to fade. When I wear purple I own the night, and all the stunning elements that embrace it.

The color purple has been tattooed on my heart; it is the core of my being.

Some may call it an obsession because I live and breathe the elegant color of purple. If purple had an aroma I believe it would be the scent of fresh vanilla and lavender. When I bathe in lavender and allow the aroma to appease my thoughts, I visualize everything in shades of purple. You see, my mindset is *'as a man thinketh so is he'*. Therefore, I see myself as royalty and I shall be treated as such and nothing less. I don't consider it arrogance or cockiness; it is just a state of mind. So do you dare to dream in purple?

Chapter Two:

My Affectionate Heart

My Guardian Angel

My guardian angel watches over me as I sleep, making sure nothing befalls me. You take me in your chiseled arms and hold me tight as I wept. Your safe arms comfort me like the wings of an eagle. As warm tears roll down my cheeks like rain, You wipe them away as only a protector could. My spirit is crushed, broken by the Beast. I feel helpless. Never once do You judge me for my mistakes but You give me promise that things will be okay.

How I yearn for this moment to never end. I feel like all of my worries and fears lose color and fade into the background. I am always such a bad judge of character; trying to see the good in people - only to be fooled. The stench of betrayal lingers as my protector whispers softly in my ear, assuring me that He will never leave my side. After all the things my protector and I have been through, He remains loyal to my needs.

When I dare say 'thank you', He gently places two fingers on my delicate lips as if to say *"this is why I'm here"*. My guardian angel helps me face my trepidations by making them seem minute. Once His work is done, my guardian angel never says goodbye. Instead, His beautiful brown eyes long to say I'm here for you, whenever you need me, as He vanishes into the still night.

Ingredients of a Man

*I'*m not a psychic; I don't have the gift of reading your mind. My lips were created to delight in the kissing game not in kissing tail. I have long legs, the color of brown sugar. They were made for walking not for spreading every time you feel an urge. I was created to be your helpmeet not your doormat. When I reviewed my resume the other day, ego stroker was not listed nor is it a hobby of mine. I search my heart in hopes of finding truth only to realize that I don't know why I love you; I just do.

I patiently wait in the background, hoping you'll find yourself. I am curious to know exactly what it is you want from me. The fact is, times-a-wasting with every second, every minute and every hour that passes. It's amazing how insecure you are but from the outside looking in no one can really tell. Life seems to do that to people especially when rejection just isn't what you are accustomed to. Even though I know this is your weakness superman, I manage to dust off your cape and give you an encouraging word so that you can fight the demons that internally torment you.

  I could go on and on about the obvious things but I have decided that what will be will be. Acceptance is what you desire but a person with an open mind is what you need. Even though you appear to be a full grown man, you possess a spirit of childlike innocence. Everyone has an inner child but how you manage that creature determines how far you get. I understand that your heart is fragile. I am aware that you should be handled with care. These are the ingredients of a man.

God's Chosen

What a mighty man of God you will be. I see you shining so bright in God's divine glory, untarnished, without blemish, because God has chosen you to be a part of His plan. How honored you must be to know that out of the millions of people God created, He chose you. He didn't want the most popular or the most likely to succeed, He wanted you - the imperfect one who has fallen short of His glory. Yes you, the one who feels unfit for the job.

If only you knew how many souls you will win for Christ. God patiently waited for the right time, pruning you like the thorough gardener He is. Making sure that you will produce the fruit that shows beneficial change. So many are lost but you will show them that there is only one road, only one way to be free.

This will not be a simple task but in God's eyes everything counts. He has an eye for your wise and willing heart that He adores so much. He chose you to encourage His people, to let them know that when all hope is gone, He'll be there. How proud of you I am indeed. When you gaze into my eyes, the reflection you'll see is the reflection of a King. As you grow in grace, always thankful, I will sit back and watch God work a wonder through you.

My Prototype

While eating my chocolate truffles, I wonder if this is what heaven is like. Every morsel is sweet to taste as the creamy mixture develops a thick mass in my mouth. The **Sweetest Taboo** plays in my ear as I watch him dress. What magnificent features he has? This man has developed in ways that can only be imagined. His posture makes so many statements but only one stands among the rest - no one has swagger like that. He is bold, brilliant in mind, and everything about him says I am paradise, come visit me please.

I quickly devour another truffle; it is so rich in flavor I feel as if there is a party going on in my mouth. He glances at me while buttoning his French cuffed shirt, preparing for another hard day's work. I think to myself, he must feel good being the boss. He sprays himself with a scent that I call the essence of a real man. The fragrance captures me, alerting all of my senses. He never says much and he doesn't have to; his eyes speak volumes. He was my angel, the one that I adore most.

Watching him is like foreplay to me. His demeanor presents strength but behind closed doors, he is as gentle as a lamb. He knows how to fill me up when I am down, turn my rainy days into blue skies. I love when he touches me; it's like the world stops turning at that very moment. Although he doesn't know it, there is no sweeter love to me than his. It was like nectar to a honey bee. I was down to my last truffle when the velvety smooth texture engrossed me. He leaned over and gave me the kiss of life. His flavor was nothing that could be found in any recipe book or seasoning. It was indescribable.

I am caught up in the rapture of him. Blessed indeed, I feel like I can conquer the world. He brings me so much joy, something I never knew existed. He had to leave my ego and all. Of course I hated to see him go but someone had to battle the fierce plantation and he was the man for the job. He cannot be duplicated because he is like no other man in the world. Consider him my prototype.

Him

I'm in love with him. I'm so in love with him. I have been swept away by his ebony embrace. I try to deny it but when I see him I get this feeling in my gut that makes me feel all funny on the inside. He knows where my head is and I can't deny it because it's written all over his face. I love this man; everything about him is my possibility. He is a behind the scenes kind of guy. He doesn't require a lot of attention because he is confident in himself.

He is not afraid to admit when he is wrong. I decided to stop looking for perfection since he is far from it. When I lowered my expectations he arrived. Through his trials he still stands tall. Although he tries to hide his pain I can see through it all. Does he know that I am in love with him? Of course he does. I can't hide all of these emotions inside; I am afraid I may explode.

I'm his orange moon and for that reason he is the light that shines through my atmosphere. He is the master piano while I am the keys to his life. With each stroke, we play an unchained melody that cannot be detained. He declares that he is not the richest man in the world, but no amount of money can replace the love I feel for him. Our souls are tied, making a unique pattern, creating the ultimate love that was created for a woman and man.

A Piece of You

    My every thought is of you. When I awaken from a peaceful sleep, I can't help but wonder what you're doing. As I lay, I pretend that you are next to me holding me tight. I don't want this moment to pass. I lie still trying to mimic your breathing. I imagine you holding me close as if it were the last. While I listen to the sultry sounds of the radio, thoughts of you consume me. My body begins to sway, becoming one with the music.

    I picture us on the dance floor, you staring at me with such intensity, never missing a beat. Your tender kisses remind me of snowflakes that gently melt away on my lips, leaving me breathless, in a daze. I gaze at my phone, hoping that if I think of you hard enough, you would feel me and make the connection. I switch roles and pretend that I am you as I slowly button your French cuffed shirt. I lightly spray your cologne in the air while I walk into the mist.

I find myself intoxicated by the scent of you as I allow it to overcome me. I miss you when you are away. I yearn for just an inkling of your touch. I long for your warm embrace as I hug my pillow, slowly drifting to a place where lovers dare to dream, hoping that when I awaken, you will be there. I am smitten with anticipation, anxiously awaiting your arrival.

Although you may leave momentarily, it seems like forever. Seconds turn into minutes, minutes into hours and hours, days. Even though you are not physically with me, I rub my protruding belly, smiling gently for you gave me the ultimate gift, a piece of you.

You

I love you deeply. As time passes, you revive me.

With all my heart, I love you so. Despite your flaws, I am determined to look beyond them. You have surpassed every expectation and probability. I find it hard to breathe, wondering if this moment will last or fade away slowly, becoming a reflection of my past. Is it a crime to think that maybe this is it - that you are the one? I love having you around. You make my day easier; the sun shines a little brighter because you are there with me. You have caused the emptiness to dissolve and you have filled my heart with an abundance of joy and gladness. Nothing about you is a façade; you are simply unique in every way. I find myself thinking of no one but you constantly. I wish you were aware of the things that were going through my head when it comes to you.

There is no mystery surrounding your love for me. The sweet things you say and do remove all doubt. With all my heart I love you. You've shown me that love conquers all, it heals all and without you in my life, love is pointless. You've shown me how to laugh again. I have a permanent glow that can be seen farther that the eyes can see. Winter no longer lives in my heart, for you have melted the frost away. I see the world clearer as it has been meticulously etched, to be admired in all its beauty. You made this possible. My summer skies are new. The love you feel for me lets me know that you will be there for me and with this love, we can conquer the world.

When I Think of You

When I think of you I think of a bold, powerful being that is strong and unmovable. I relish in the way you listen and take in everything I say as if you own the language I speak. You don't claim to be the most knowledgeable but you do attempt to get an understanding. Diligence comes to mind when I think of you, not so much as a perfectionist but one who has a constant push for order. This asset is astonishing to me.

I tend to shy away when you are near me; your slightest touch makes me just tingle inside. I desire to always be at my best when I am around you. I want to appear perfect in your eyes but I know that isn't possible, for I am only human. When you look, I get the impression that you can strip me down and see my vulnerability and my soul. I feel naked and exposed. I wonder if you could accept me for who I truly am and not the "Miss

Independent," always strong, put together woman that I attempt to be.

Could it be that someone who demands so much respect, someone who is so secure within himself could have a sensitive side and be my comfort zone? Could he let me peel away the layers that contain a broken heart and allow me to help him heal? These are the questions that preoccupy my mind when I look into your eyes. These exquisite eyes that are elegant in detail hide the joys and pains of life. These eyes seek acceptance along with the desire for closure.

These eyes are the windows to a mystifying soul. I love your laughter; it excites me. It makes me feel like I did that, I made that happen. No one else can make you laugh or put that smile on your face like me. You are my forbidden fruit, my hidden treasure, my confidant, my best friend.

My Friend

My friend is the one who causes my heart to skip a beat every time I bask in his presence. Who knew that friendship could be so sweet? I indulge in its feast as I try to savor the flavor of all its fine delicacies. This friend of mine is like none other, always consistent and true, loyal till the end. We have a bond that cannot be broken; he tells me the truth even though it may pierce my tender feelings. I appreciate his honesty and that is what holds our friendship together like glue.

Without honesty, our friendship would be meaningless. A friendship without basis is destined to fail. My friend is so real; I don't have to put on airs to be around him. Since he is so comfortable in his own skin, I can let my guard down. This man makes it easy for me to be me and it feels good to be free with him. We sometimes agree to disagree which is to be expected because friendship is a process. He reassures me that our friendship is worth the time, and investment that won't ever need a bailout plan.

Loving him is effortless because it comes so naturally. We are like two peas in a pod, frick & frack, ying & yang, Bonnie & Clyde, my partner in crime. When I see him I see me. Our friendship has endless possibilities and in all of our endeavors my friend will be ever so careful to look out for me because that is what a true friend does. I couldn't ask for anything more ….my friend….you know who you are.

Melody of the Heart

I hear an acoustic song playing in the air. A melody so sweet, it brings tears to my eyes. This tune is familiar. It reminds me of my first love for music. Without it, I would surely die. I desperately seek the origin of the sound. The closer I get, the faster the tempo. The range could only be described as beautiful. I find myself delighting in the harmony, humming the tune as if I were apart of its symphony. I wasn't surprised when I learned that a sound so superb could only come from the depths of the heart. A melody derived from the heart of a man causes that man to desire to be more like Him.

Chapter Three:

My Loathing Heart

Heartless Ways of Man

It is what it is and it is what it will be. Disgusted with all of the pretending, all of the disguises. Why can't people put all of the fakeness aside and just be real? All of the foolishness, all of the games, why can't I just accept the way the game of life is played. Jealousy, envy, deceit, and greed all seem to be apart of the human race who hides behind the masks of deception. I have struggled to bypass the heartless ways of man but I continue to come up short each and every time. I've learned that the deceitful heart will always exist, hidden behind the tears of a clown.

Is it fair to seek perfection? In my heart I wrestle with my expectations of knowing the ordinary just won't do. Being used and taken advantage of is an unsolved cold case of my empathy. Is this reality or simply life uncovering my blinded eyes to help me see that people are not what I perceive them to be? It is a daily struggle for me to grow wiser and process the fact that no one will treat me the way I desire.

If you could see through my unadulterated eyes you would find what lies in the soul of man will come out in due time. I haven't given up; I have decided to take a step back allowing, myself to fade into the background, analyzing the mistreatment of my good will. I realize that I have been living in a pastime paradise in hopes that humanity would turn from their evil ways. I live, desiring to be freed from the inevitable, watching the signs of the times as they continue to unravel. Do I stand alone? I wish that we could learn to love each other as one. Only then will this world become a better place.

Where Has All The Romance Gone?

Where has all the romance gone? Whatever happened to expressing yourself, especially if it's from the heart? I am saddened by the fact that romance no longer exists. Maybe I am just a hopeless romantic. I find myself searching for romance to no avail. Why must I be so passionate, so different and desirous of something that isn't feasible? I was told men were raised to be strong, to be protectors, to be providers. I was told that men were taught not to express themselves, to hold in their tears because that is a sign of weakness.

What is so wrong with a man being in touch with his inner feelings? I have yet to find the crime in a man having a sensitive side. What's wrong with a man showing that he is indeed human? How immoral is it for a man to cry? Will a man loose his soul if he sheds a single tear? Crying is a gift given to man by God. When life drops its heavy load upon his shoulders, he will desperately seek a release.

If man refuses to cry, how can God wipe all of his tears away? This one, fragmented emotion only shows that man has a heart and is willing to allow God into his heart to soothe and comfort as only a true Sovereign would. The question still remains: where has all the romance gone? Perhaps if I try a little harder to visualize the church being romantically involved with God, then maybe one day romance can be greater than before.

Holiday Blues

I do dread the holidays and all of its commercialism. The world has twisted its true meaning into something that is totally sickening and distorted. Whatever happened to the true significance of family? I recall times of being so excited about family gatherings and so eager to benefit from the home cooked meals that I could hardly contain myself. Times have changed, people have changed and things are not the same.

I have become aware of family secrets which have taken the intimacy of family from me.
I am baffled by the idea that the world has placed on its network to try and make us thing we need certain merchandise regardless of the devastation the economy is in. I find it hard to decorate for the season because my sweet innocence shelters me from the ways of the world. I

heard a singer emphasize that this world needs love but I beg to differ because love can't heal all wounds.

I see homeless people in the streets, begging for help of any kind while the rich mishandle money as if they have money making institutions in their backyards. The Bible states that the meek shall inherit the earth but my heart grows weary while it attempts to run a race that apparently can't be won. The world is so deceitful with all of its wickedness, promoting death like a $2 whore in the streets.

Who would have ever thought that a time would come when one could buy a gift card for an abortion? Are we so hard up that we have lost sight of what is really important? Whatever happened to promoting life? Instead of promoting life, man has promoted the idea of playing God by inventing something as immoral as cloning. It is evident that the end is near. But the real question is will you be ready when it's here?

Chapter Four:

My Sensual Heart

Sexual Appetite

𝒫atiently waiting. Anxiously waiting. All I can do is touch myself until that time comes. I inhale. I exhale. I try to cool down this internal fire that burns inside me. I send my cookies via text message, letting you know my carnal thoughts, making you aware that this is slippery when wet. I sent you a picture [via text] so that you can visualize how enticing my inner thighs are. I want to be treated as if I were an all you can eat buffet.

𝒥know you can handle this and I just need you to satisfy this fierce appetite I have. I only crave you, your tender touch. You know my hot spots, even the ones that I have yet to explore. You are my motivation. When I am at work I have to constantly stay on my grind because the thought of you makes me want to do you. I fantasize about the warmth of your tongue tickling my clit, hoping that maybe you would make it feel like vapors when you blow gently to make her purr. Ooooh meow.

I just want you to give it to me the way you always do big daddy. Nothing is predictable when it comes down to our sexual escapades. This is why I can't help but come back for more. Your name should be addiction because I am your addict. You are so good that the thought of you touching someone else makes my brown eyes turn emerald green with jealousy. You belong to me, and I don't wanna share. It's like an inferno baby. I wish that you would submerge into me until we become one.

*C*an I be your student? I want you to teach me because I want to make an "A". "A" simply stands for anal [sex] - which requires extra credit in order to pass your course. Graduation is what I need to maintain my position in your erotic city. I imagine us role playing. I'm your naughty girl. Therefore, I will do whatever it takes for you to get me back in line. If you want to blindfold me, bind my hands, I am down with anything to get back in your good graces. I will be your lover, your sex slave, your whore. Wherever, whenever, anytime and anyplace.

The Art of Making Love

The way we touched was magnetic. The intensity was like an electric current when he penetrated my sugar walls. He made sure to be ever so careful while he kissed the nape of my neck with his soft lips. He pinned my arms back as if I were his sex slave. He began to explore my body with his tongue. His tongue danced around my nipples as if they were his chocolate fantasy.

My moans indicated he could continue. I attempted to hold back as long as I could but that was impossible. The pleasure I felt was so intense; I had never felt this way before. His tongue continued to travel to my wonderland of desire. My body began to tremble, matching the rhythm of the flickering candle that burned bright, exposing my femininity.

He took delight in how I tried to escape his strong hold. Again, I moaned; not in pain but because of the vast enjoyment. I was rendered powerless as I felt his tongue inside my love. I began to loose my cool. The feeling was indescribable. I knew that I had been deprived. But he was willing to take his time with me as only a real man would. I was lost in a sea of emotions as tears ran down my face.

He kissed my tears while he whispered so sweetly in my ear "I love you". He pulled and teased me, giving just a little at a time. He allowed me to take control as I pushed him on his back. Pleasing him was effortless. I embraced all of him with my mouth. I spoke softly in his mic, "I am going to teach you a lesson."

As I continued to engulf him with my warm, oral hollow space, he groaned while caressing my head with his hands. I straddled him as if to say, you're mine now. I guided him inside my abyss that only fit his mold. He knew this was his. I reassured him with every stroke. His anatomy captivated me so I focused on it. He smiled as I kissed his forehead intimately. He pulled me close to his chest while he drove himself inside me vigorously. We exploded at once.

In my mind I could see all of the colors of love as he released himself inside me. This time was different. Emotions were on another level. I laid my head on his chest and listened to him breathe, knowing that he was satisfied. As we drifted to sleep, I whispered to him "I love you." He is mine. I am his. We are one.

Chapter Five:

My Longing Heart

Fallen

Who would have ever thought that I would have fallen so quickly? I tried, with no avail to keep my guard up. But every time you came around, you managed to melt away the lock and key that hid my wounded heart with your sincere love for me. You continue to help me step out the box with my emotions. Instead of my emotional bank being overdrawn, you have made a deposit that is life altering.

You've allowed me to see the world differently. Where I viewed love through rose colored glasses, you have removed them and allowed me to regain focus and learn from my past. I have finally faced reality and realized that time was wasting. I needed to live and let go. I pray daily, thanking God for you.

I can't begin to tell you how overjoyed I am that God allowed you into my life. When I was in despair, God was listening, molding you into the man that He knew I needed. As I sit here I think on the good times that we've shared and how I look forward to the future knowing that I have so much to look forward to. You are my joy, my reckless love. With you, there are no boundaries. And with you, I see no end.

The Power of Love

The heart is something very powerful but it can't protect itself from life's ups and downs. The beating of my heart yearns to be loved. It seems to beat faster and pump harder when it is stroked by this intense feeling. There isn't a feeling more desirable than to know that someone loves you. To be deeply in love is something indescribable. When you receive a dozen roses on the job by someone who is declaring their love for you to the world, it's amazing.

When you find yourself racing home just to be with the one you are so deeply in love with, it's like the anticipation of closing on your first home. To be so in tune with a person that you finish each other's sentences, to know your thoughts are their thoughts is amazing. How I yearn to be in love? The way his hands move when he is undressing me, carefully savoring every moment as if he wants time to stand still. The way my body feels, wanting him to just grace me with his touch over and over again until I lose control.

When in love, only his presence satisfies the hunger that burns inside of me. Only he can persuade me to do the unthinkable. How I yearn to be in love? What a wonderful sensation I get just by wearing his t-shirt, longing for his smell to engulf me with his essence when he is away. Is it a surprise that love could be so sweet? The heart is something very powerful but it can't protect itself from the pain that it may endure. Only love is a plausible cure. Love cures all things. Even in the heart's worse state, the power of love will always stand strong.

Love and I

Love and I have a bittersweet relationship that is simply impossible to explain. Sometimes Love is my best friend; we can talk about almost anything. Love sees me for who I am even though I am not perfect; he is very accepting. Love holds me tight, never letting me go although he knows it's because of him that I cry. We sit back and reminisce on how I never consult my fragile heart. I go into situations, blinded by my attempts to save the world. He argues the fact that everyone doesn't deserve a piece of what we share. He assures me that he will always be there to catch me when I fall.

Love has a way of distancing himself when he feels that he is overstepping his boundaries. He goes his way and I go mine. I never look back as I parade off in anger, leaving my friend behind. What hurts me the most about Love is that it's obvious how I feel about him and it's apparent he feels the same way too. It just pains me to be patient long enough to see what Love has in store for me. Love is tricky; he continues to give off mixed signals. He swears that he means no harm but in the end he realizes the mess that he has made; he's unintentionally created an enemy.

  Love and I have had our share of ups and downs but he always finds a place back into my heart. We have laughed and cried together in spite of our differences. Even though Love was inhabited by someone else when I found him, he still found time to dwell inside of me. Love is what you make of him. I just wish he could understand that I only want him as a friend; I yearn for him to be the peace within. Without Love, I'm incomplete, not whole, and half empty. One day I hope that we can simply find Love again.

Between You & Me

Time passes by like the sand in an hourglass. The day turns into night like summer descends into fall. Things continue to change around me but my love for you remains. I tried to move on with my life, expecting memories of you to disappear. My love for you only grew stronger. I must have been a fool, thinking there was an "easy button" for all of these emotions. I was told that you haven't learned the true meaning of love until you get hurt and that's how you know you're doing it right. Even in our darkest times, the light from our love is always illuminating, making a tripod of color that could not be named.

I called you my prototype, sure that no one could duplicate you in all of your grandeur. Is it possible that I am the female version of you? I laugh to myself when I think of the private jokes we share. I miss you so, my best friend, the one who knows me more than I know myself.

When we are apart I feel as if I've lost my soul. I am just an empty vessel and only your love can fill me up. You are the only medicine that can cure my ailing heart.

It's strange how things reveal themselves over time. The truth is, you have always had my heart and I have always tried to fight the obvious. Nothing compares to you or ever will for that matter. I have made up in my mind that right now is the time and this is how I feel about this vibe between you and me.

The Way I See Love Through You

I have never felt this before. I cherish every moment that we share as if it were our last. I thought that love didn't exist until I met you. You helped me regain the courage to let my guard down, to allow love to take flight. I have finally recognized that without you, I am nothing. In you I find contentment. There is no other man that I want, need or desire.

You are the spoken word that comes from my heart. Without you my gift would go unheard. I turn to you to save me from myself. When my days seem dark, you are the light of my world. I have a love hangover so strong that the only cure is you. There are no limits to the love that we share. When I'm with you I feel an overflow that my body cannot contain. Our chemistry is magnetic. It cultivates an atmosphere that only true lovers can explain.

I am the beautiful rose standing tall while you are the soil that assists in nurturing me. Without the soil, the rose would not exist. I've been told that I live inside a fantasy world but what would love be like if imagination did not exist. I love the idea of love and every aspect of it. If I had not met you, I would have never experienced love in its entirety. Some people see love in black and white but I see love in multifaceted color. This is the way I see love through you.

Brown Eyes

*B*rown eyes that give off so much mystery.

Brown eyes that determine hurt, pain, disgust, happiness, anguish and joy. The eyes of the beholder who I hold close to my heart. These beautiful brown eyes were designed with such diligence. The detail is so splendid that I wonder what life is like seen through those brown eyes. The color is like nothing I have ever seen before. I wonder if the painter mixed all of the glorious colors of brown to create such a warm and unique shade that appears like iridescence in the sunlight.

*P*riceless comes to mind when I see these elegant and rare brown eyes. It's as if they were designed from hand blown glass. When I look into these remarkable brown eyes, I see serenity. I find myself so drawn to these brown eyes as if they cast a spell on me. Brown eyes, oh how you intrigue me? I love it when the beholder undresses me with his eyes. It's like being enveloped by the warmth of a wood fire on a cold winter's day. They do not judge me. They see my flaws but are curious to know more. The beholder's gaze penetrates my soul.

If these brown eyes could see the inner me, what would they see? Would they see my wounded heart? Would they see years and years of abandonment, hurt and pain? Would they see a defenseless, shy little girl who longs for acceptance? Once these brown eyes discover my secret, would they see me in the same light? Or would they cast me away in disgust, repulsed by what lies beneath? These brown eyes prevent me from seeing the beholder's inner man although the eyes are the window to the soul. Brown eye: so brilliant and refined; my most valued treasure; the epitome of my desire.

God's Gift to Me

Loving you is so easy to do. It's like connecting the dots. Our chemistry is amazing. I feel that we have known each other for a lifetime. Are we soul mates? This is how I feel when I am with you. You make me so happy, happy that you chose me. He who findeth a wife findeth a good thing. The picnics in the park, the candle lit dinners, or just holding hands gives me chills because I knew that you were meant for me. I prayed for you and God gave you to me, my gift, my joy, my husband.

It took some time but it was well worth the wait. When we slow dance to our favorite song, I think of all the wonderful things that are in store. How I can't wait to give you the son that you yearn for. I can't wait to see the joy in your eyes when we conquer the world together - just you and me.

I just love you so, my king, the love of my life.

How I cherish and adore you? Nothing can change how I feel. Loving you is so carefree, natural in a sense, just so easy to do.

In Love with You

*R*oses are red; violets are blue; I knew that it would feel so good to be in love with you. You bring so much happiness and joy into my life. When I am out and about, I find myself humming a song that only my heart can provide the rhythm to. You are my strong black Nubian King, aspiring to be all that I need. When I need comforting, you are there to shelter me from the rain. When I am in pain, you encourage the sun to shine down on me with all of its warmth and pleasant rays.

I love being in love with you. In your arms is where I belong as I lay my head on your chest. There, I find security and strength. This is where I belong. You can always find a way to make me feel as beautiful as a distant sunset over the ocean. As you caress my face you stare deep into my eyes, declaring how much you desire me. You are as much apart of me as I am apart of you.

When I see you going through the struggles of life, I secretly pray that God covers your mind. I massage your temples in hopes of relieving the pressure. You belong to me and it is my duty to protect you from any harm that may cause your spirit to be wounded. When you make passionate love to me it is as if the world has stopped rotating on its axis. Money doesn't matter when I am with you. The time you spend with me is satisfying enough.

I love you and only you. I am so in love, it is almost pathetic but I don't care. Love only comes once in a lifetime so why not make the most of it? I cherish every moment that we share ,as if it were our last; I am in love with you. There will be hard times to come but in time, love will show and prove that it conquers all. I love you unconditionally, no matter the circumstance. I will fight to make things work because my love is true. Roses are red; violets are blue; I will shout it from the hilltops that I am in love with you.

The Setup

She watches him carefully, making sure she doesn't miss a beat. She listens to him, being ever so careful to catch every word as if it were manna falling from heaven. He tries to downplay certain aspects of himself because he hasn't quite figured out that she is oh so clever and sees right through it. Everything right now is fresh and new, not so much a game but a matter of feeling each other. While studying his gestures, she wonders what makes him truly tick. Will he allow her to be the beautiful black butterfly that she truly is?

He is such the super hero. But the lingering question is when he takes off his cape can she love him for who he is? Beyond his exterior, he requires a different kind of love, an unconditional love. He watches her precisely, making sure not to be obvious. It's hard because she intrigues him. He desires security in knowing that if times were hard she could be his armor while in battle.

He presents strength but she understands that he is human in every kind of way. She is careful not to jump in so quickly because the situation isn't as easy as it appears to be. She prefers to let time handle her light weight. They both sit back, analyzing each other, wondering what lies ahead for them. This moment sets the tone. No obligations. No worries. The idea of enjoying the moment and taking it for what it is can only be defined as priceless.

Love of My Life

I wanna share my every waking moment with you because you give me strength. You give me the ability to strive for more. You are my encourager, my motivator, the one I can always turn too. When I had doubts, you came along and showed me anything was possible if I just believed. You told me that I was beautiful when I couldn't see past my scars. You showed me kindness and mercy when I didn't show you an ounce of remorse in the delivery of my anger.

I know I can depend on you in my time of need. You have showed me numerous times that when all else fails, you will be there. You always kept the lines of communication open even when you didn't agree with my actions. For that, I love you. You are truly amazing. A blessing in disguise. A good man who is humble. A man of integrity. Yes, that you are. I dare not put you on a pedestal for my God is a jealous God. I thank God for allowing me to experience a gift so genuine that only He could have provided this for me.

You've helped me to pick up the pieces when I felt as if my world had crumbled. You love me in a special way, looking past the human side of me and just loving me for the imperfect being that I am. Some words are so hard to say but you can interpret my emotions without me saying a word. I can accomplish countless things but without you by my side, my life would be incomplete. What good would it be to have all the pleasures in life if you were not there to share them with me? You are the love of my life.

Story of My Life

I take pleasure in admiring the entity that causes me to feel overwhelmed on the inside. My soul's purpose is not to be discovered as I take in every fragment of his being. His masculinity is the quintessence of sexy. Words cannot describe his swagger. Only the tune of the piano that plays in my head describes it. Only the sensual sounds of bass that pulsates through my small frame with every step he takes describe it. I desire to know what he smells like but I am too afraid to approach him.

I can only imagine the intoxicating fragrance that would inhabit my senses, leaving me helpless, overtaken by such intensity. His laid back demeanor, which draws me into a tangled web of curiosity, is clever. It seems as though he enjoys taking in everything around him then decides if he will include himself in the arena of life. I call him the "observant one". He is a man of few words but when he speaks the words seem to roll off his tongue effortlessly.

Like morning dew drops, his presence refreshes my soul. In passing I catch a quick glimpse of him careful not to stare. As his lips part to speak to me, I peer into his eyes only to see a silent story that only he can tell. I begin to speak but only silence, only air and only fear escape my lips. Could this really be happening to me? My intentions were to say something but I just walked on while he passed by. In my heart all I could think was he noticed me once again.

The saga plays out the same each day like a rerun of my favorite soap opera. I plan to muster up enough courage to speak but I am tormented by this caged shyness, missing my opportunity with a man who seems to be destined for me, the man of my dreams. This is the story of my life.

Declaration of Love

What is it when you're so in love with a person that no matter what they do, you love them anyway? I don't expect to be with the richest of the rich but I do expect to be comfortable. I don't expect for you to be perfect because I'm not looking for perfection. Is it so hard to believe that I'm on fire for you? I think it is an honor to be adored and not allow superficial things to get in the way of this unconditional love that I feel for you. The moment that I looked into your eyes I saw my forever.

When we touch, I can feel my guard melting away, exposing my vulnerability. You tell me things that allow me to think. I anticipate hearing the knowledge that rolls off your tongue with ease. You correct me with love being careful not to cause strife. A wise man I have found. Or did you find me? I hum melodious tunes because you have given me a new song to sing. I can remember when we first made the connection. It was as if a light bulb went off, shining ever so brightly indicating that you were the one.

You are special to me and this is why I desire to be purified, cleansed, untainted, and undefiled. I desire to be made over again which is a process that takes time and effort. Every moment with you is an occasion and it feels so right. You are the poem that derives from my heart, the thread that helps me hold it together, the comforter that I yearn for when things seem intimidating. You are who you are and nothing more. Only one person can be number one in my life and you don't mind that because second place is better than none.

I can't help you got me because you are truth. You meet me half way since you're not afraid to compromise. I have no restraint when expressing my deepest feelings for you, whether through poetry, music or just a gentle gesture of gratitude. You have given me a reason to live life to the fullest. Because of you, I believe in the power of love and all there is to follow. For once, without hesitation, I have the ability to say I love you and only you. Then, I exhale.

Deep Thought

I sit and wonder what my life will be like with you.

Questions flood my mind, with hope that as each day goes by, you will answer them for me. Not just by your kind words but by your sincere actions. I watch you out of curiosity, longing to know what your thoughts are. Is your story simple or complicated? Oh, how I desire to know more? Everything about you intrigues me, from your sense of humor down to your sense of compassion.

*C*ould you be the answer to my prayers? I have so many questions but I have come to the conclusion that what will be, will be. It seems that you have so many layers, layers of hurt, pain and sorrow. But the closer I get, I notice underneath the scaring, there is hope. Even though you have been wounded, I intend to peel away the damage and make you new again.

When I am around you I feel your intensity. You yearn to be loved. Would it be such a crime to wanna love you back? I admire the complexion of your skin and how truly beautiful it is. The color renders me speechless. Is it true what they say "the blacker the berry the sweeter the juice'? I call you my chocolate delight, my mahogany desire.

I ponder what it would feel like to be held by you. The slightest touch from you causes all of my suppressed emotions to be revealed. When you look at me I feel so much passion and desire. I hope that what we create will be a reflection of what God intended love between a man and a woman to be.

Chapter Six:

My Devoted Heart

My Secret Place

Tears roll down my face, burning my skin like a wildfire. I seek shelter as I run to hide from the grief and obvious pain that I feel. Resentment has made a place in my heart like death inhabits the cemetery. My vision is blurred as I am unable to focus or find meaning behind the agony that has saturated my very being. I want to be set free from this bondage that tortures my soul.

I dwell in my hiding place, avoiding the embarrassment that encompasses me. I don't want to appear weak but my spirit is broken, embraced by torment that whispers solemnly in my ear. I find myself going in circles as I thirst for strength to overcome my pain. My tears are a release but I am ashamed of the vulnerability that comes with it. I want to be comforted by someone with understanding and compassion in their heart. I have yet to find that one.

I find ease in my secret place, yet I am still alone.

This is a terrible feeling but I sense that Your love is near. I desire to be healed while I have been wounded by life's struggles. I attempt to leave the darkness that occupies my mind. The tears continue to linger, creating a miniature river that filters my sorrows. I recoil from pity. I need Your love to infiltrate me. I crave for Your love to shine like a light to restore life that has been sucked away by turmoil and stress.

I feel Your presence as I turn around. I see Your face. You are more beautiful than I envisioned. Lord, it's me, the one who is so unworthy and unfaithful. Yet, You take me into Your arms. I struggle to hold back my tears as You console me. I cling to You as You began to wipe my tears away, making them Your own. You whisper softly that You will never leave me. You will always find your way back in my life no matter how I attempt to hide. I rise leaving my frustrations, anxieties and pain in my secret place with my Father. He came to me and lifted all my burdens just like He promised. Now I am renewed.

Who Made the Rules to Praising God?

It's so hard to do right. There are so many rules and regulations for living saved. Being a Christian is a full-time job in itself. It's even more difficult when others are watching your every move. How you handle a situation almost determines if you will win a soul for Christ or cause someone to believe that all Christians are the same. A hypocrite in sheep clothing is what I call them.

It's not right to question God but sometimes that is very hard to do. God has put us all here for a reason and that is to be fruitful, be an example and show those that doubt Him that life is greener on the other side of salvation. It's so easy to sign up and fight for a country that is heartless and unforgiving but so hard to sign up and join a fight in that gives one peace and satisfaction in knowing that their fight is not in vain.

Oh the decisions that we must make: do I live right or fall into the hands of the devil, continually tricked and deceived by his lies? The choice is yours to make. Remember when you face God, you will face Him alone.

Companionship

I found myself a friend who knows me well. As I walk along, He holds my hand to guide my walk. I find comfort in Him as I stroll down this twisted road called life. He allows me to make mistakes as I set out on my journey, not discouraged about falling but determined to learn from each experience and encounter. When I have difficulty sleeping, He is there waiting, eagerly listening to what troubles me. We have the most in depth conversations. He tells me how He knew me before He formed me in my mother's womb. He goes on to explain how He set me apart, appointing me to do His business.

As we continue walking hand in hand, He allows me to walk in His shoes, showing me the things that He sees. Along the way, He invites me to His house. I find delight in our fellowship for He is the bread of life. I always wondered what it would feel like to be loved immensely. But it's not a secret anymore; He sees the best in me. I am His orange moon. When others see me, they see a vessel consumed by a beacon of light that reflects Him. I am growing in grace, blessed by His divine glory.

I am touched deep in my soul from being with Him. He uplifts me when I'm down. When I feel less than beautiful, He whispers to me that I am created in His image. He tells me how the seasons may change but His undying love for me remains the same. He is the great "I am"; I wouldn't trade Him for all the wealth in the world because He is heir of all things. If you don't know Him, I strongly suggest that you get to know Him. There is no greater love than His. He is my all and all; He helps me when I fall. He is dear to me: my creator, my shepherd and overseer. With Him, there are endless possibilities and no limitations. He is the way, the truth and the light. I would certainly be lost without Him.

The Truth of the Matter is ...

When you go looking for things, don't be upset about what you find. You can't change people and if you must attempt it, I suggest you start at their birth. I have succeeded at putting people in places where they don't deserve to be and I believe that I am not the only one guilty of this maneuver. Only one sits on a pedestal in my heart and that is Jesus Christ Himself. When I tried to substitute, I was highly disappointed. I was gravely mistaken thinking that integrity, character, trust and humility could be found amongst people.

I understand that God is working on others, just like He is working on me because I am nowhere near perfect. But to deliberately plot to undermine an individual is unacceptable. I am tired of the deviant behavior that I observe on a daily basis. I am tired of people using their insecurities as a crutch, trying to hurt others because they really don't know who they are or what they want out of life. I have also realized that some people are just pawns for the devil and their whole intent and sole purpose in life is to manipulate, plot and scheme to keep others from being happy.

I am tired of loosing sleep over things that are beyond my control. So my mindset is *'let go and let God'*. My rivers have run dry and I'm all cried out from expecting people to be something that I think they should be or treat me the way I feel I should be treated. It's time to press on and consider my daily trials a lesson learned. I will not continue a mental pity party, desiring things that are clearly not for me. I am not going to give people that much power over me. It's a new day to trust God and if it's a fight that you want, I will give you what you are looking for because I have the right person on my side. Do you know Him?

Duet 6:5

*H*ere is my heart Lord, I give my all to You. I've made up my mind that You are the light that can restore, renew and make me whole again. Tears fall as I sit and think about the things that You have brought me through. How can I deprive You of my presence when all you ask of me is intimacy, like that between a father and his child? Your love is like none I've ever known.

*E*ven in my rebellious state You provide agape love. The only thing that is constant in my life is You. When my heart was broken, You mended it by your stripes. I can tell the world that it was Your saving grace that kept me. When I felt all hope was gone, You poured out love that soothed me like lavender, like therapy for my soul. You give me strength in times of trouble. Like an orchestra without a director or a piano without keys, I would be lost without Your presence in my life. Like a waterfall, I want You to fall fresh on me. Lord, fill my heart with Your love so that others can see You in me. I want to be more like You; I want to be pleasing in Your sight. I pray You never take your hands off me and with Your love, my purpose can take flight.

My Love

My love is the truth and the light; allow me to set you free. Many have tried to duplicate my love, not understanding that there is only one; it cannot be reproduced. My love is filtered, the purest that can be found; it has no limits, accepting the perfect imperfection. My love is an open book, illustrating passion and desire that will not falter. My love is not an illusion, but many have become intoxicated by its very essence, not really understanding its true meaning. My love has depth like the promise of a rainbow after the storm.

My love is stronger than pride. Those who have experienced my love can attest that it is addictive, after realizing that only I can satisfy their inner thirst. My love is especially customized to fit whatever your heart is in need of - whether healing, growth or southern comfort. My love can drive a rational man insane because he underestimates its power. My love is fragile and when you are in its presence, you must handle it with care. If you do not heed the warning, my love can cause pain so intense, it will cut you like a two edged sword.

My love is simple, not requiring much. It is second to none. Like the sun rises, my love grows, engaging in all of the wonderful colors of the world. My love has no boundaries. My love is colorblind; it only sees the matters of the heart. My love consists of all of these things but the reality is if it wasn't for Him I would be lost. Without Him I would be seeking love from one who is undeserving. Once I found His love, everything else followed. He is my first love as I am His. We are one.

He Is

I's time to leave the excess baggage behind.

Goodbye. Goodbye. It's draining so much out of me. I tried to understand it all. Sitting silently, hoping to hear a word. But none was uttered. I dream dreams. I understand some: they are right on point and direct, guiding me the way I should go. Others though are unclear and confusing. It still amazes me to look in the mirror and see a reflection of something I would like to call beauty. I just know that love is on its way. I no longer see a broken heart. I see my sprit being crafted from sand to polished glass. I am no longer an exquisite china doll with the painted face. What you see now is someone who is made over.

I am the rose growing through concrete soil, ever realizing that I shouldn't have overcome my obstacles. Yet, through grace and mercy, I withstood it all. Like an earthquake, my world hasn't been just lightly stirred, but shaken to the core. If you only knew the things that I see. My persona was like the blackest lily but He came and embraced me with the kiss of life. I didn't have to pretend to be happy anymore because it felt like the rain washed all of my despair away. His nectar is the sweetest I have ever tasted and it's addictive; I keep coming back for more.

  I just wanna be closer to Him because He keeps me going in the right direction. Oooooh his love is soooo good. He is so into me. More than anyone I have been with, I try to please Him in every way possible. When He beckons for me, I run to my secret closet, anticipating the wisdom He wants to share with me. I have never been in love like this before. When I am down, He gives me beautiful days with perfect blue skies. He serenades me with the melodies of the humming birds. I will never give Him up because He loves me unconditionally, flaws and all, the good and the bad. He is the best part of waking up and He is the best thing that ever happened to me.

Chapter Seven:

Aching Heart

Still Addicted

It took me a minute to gather myself and pick my pride up off the floor. What you said crushed my spirits. It was as if cement was being poured over my heart. Every word that you uttered out of your mouth caused my heart to become hard. The only thing that registered was the rejection. As it began to settle, I was a wreck on the inside. I succeeded in not allowing you to read me. I no longer wear my emotions on my sleeve. You couldn't see past the blank stare that I mastered in dealing with all the hurt you continue to bring me.

I have come to the realization that hurt people do in fact hurt people. I keep hearing that soft voice in my spirit whisper "he's not ready." I was trying to hold back the tears that welled up in my eyes. I began to thank God for the invention of sunglasses for without them, you would be able to see that I was slowly loosing control. I stood there allowing your hurtful words to penetrate my heart like salt being poured onto an open wound. Normally, I would have a comeback, but this time, I remained silent.

My only response was "ok". While my heart was bleeding, I felt as if I just witnessed a massacre. As you hugged me, I wanted to cry like a baby. I tried pushing you away but you weren't having it. I have been a victim of so many lies and so much deceit I could feel the pressure weighing on me like a ton of bricks. I whisper softly "let me go" but you respond "I'm not ready to let you go". I forced you, as I walked away damaged once again. The question that still remains is how is it possible that I'm still in love with you?

Beauty & the Beast

Everything about him was different, so she thought. The gentleman was all that she thought she needed: provider, comforter, comedian and father figure to the children. Indeed she was mistaken. Why was she such a poor judge of character? All the signs were there but she thought that love would heal him from his past. Beauty was her name. She was the epitome of just that. It was very rare to find someone who was beautiful inside and out. She always had a way of making the best out of a seemingly bad situation. Beauty thought that she could save the world when indeed she would end up having to save herself.

The gentleman was delightful at times. But when faced with hardship he had no way of controlling his rage. He would transform into the vicious Beast that would challenge anyone that tried to get close to him. The gentleman was angry about so many things. A broken individual indeed; his life was not all sunshine and rainbows. The gentleman spoke of betrayal and deceit. He talked of never being able to really trust anyone. Beauty would comfort him. She thought that she was the only one that could protect him from such devastation. When the Beast came out, she was the only one who could calm him.

The Beast would cry out, Beauty would tend to the Beast like a shepherd to his sheep. Beauty was there to cry with him and help him deal with his struggles. Beauty would express to him that he was the greatest gift of her life. She would hold him until the Beast was calmed. Beauty's love for the gentleman was not enough. Beauty didn't realize that his hurts were deeper than she imagined. As time passed, the Beast was not easily subdued. His anger was so profound that Beauty began to fear for her safety. The gentleman was now just a figment of her imagination. The Beast was her reality and there was no escaping him without loosing her life.

Beauty's future was very clear to her as she began to paint the picture. The picture revealed that she would die indeed. The Beast would take her and strip her of her pride. Her graceful smile would be hidden under the disfigurement of scraps and bruises. Sadly, Beauty will stay to the end, hoping that she is able to tame the gentleman's inner beast. But to no avail. Beauty is defeated, loving the gentleman more than her self and dying by the rage of his inner Beast. What Beauty failed to realize is that only the gentleman could save himself; he was his own worse enemy.

The Effects of Love

I am so hurt! When I open my mouth to speak nothing comes out, not a sound. I heard that love is the cure but it's actually a curse. It makes me cry uncontrollably; it makes me have countless, sleepless nights. At one point in my life, I loved the idea of love and being in love with someone who could reflect the same love that I gave so freely. Love has left me wounded, all swollen on the inside, full of grief.

I don't attend funerals but I will be the first in line to bury love and the scars it has left me with. Love set me up for failure. The good ole' days when love broke the mold and brought joy in desperate times are gone. Love tricked me. I didn't know how deceit felt until we met. Love left my heart damaged beyond repair from the constant neglect.

It's devastating to love someone who doesn't love you in return. No matter how hard you try, your all just isn't good enough. My heart is in foreclosure; love left my heart abandoned, lost and all I can do is fade into the background. I lay here nightly thinking, analyzing and wondering what I could have done to change my outcome. But nothing comes to mind. I never knew how the sting of betrayal could feel until I found love.

Love held me hostage but once I was set free, I was delusional and unfit for the world because the burden of love was too much. Who will save me from myself? I lay here wondering if I'm even worth saving as I cry myself to sleep once again with the stench of love on my breath in hopes that it will just let me be to wither away in the darkness my heart holds.

Confessions of the Soul

I remember the confession like it was yesterday.

It's amazing how a little secret can turn into torment. The torment seems to eat away at his soul. He talked of sleepless nights, unbearable nightmares and waking up in cold sweats. The thought of him suffering appeased me. Now he could clearly understand my devastation, my pain and my mental anguish. I waited for time to take its toll on him because if I handled it, it would not be pretty.

I'm cold on the inside; my heart is frozen. Love used to exist here but not anymore. It's a frigid, excruciating pain that I have endured for what seems like a lifetime. Why did it take him so long to just be honest? Didn't he know that I would still love him regardless? Unconditional love, does that ring a bell? This love still exists. I thought that I had proven myself worthy of his trust but it is evident that I failed once again. He always complained of his past hurt and pain. Who cares? Everybody has been through something; that's what makes the world go around.

Tears rolled down his cheeks. I wondered if they were tears of guilt or tears of sincere sorrow requesting forgiveness. I searched my heart for an ounce of empathy but I came up empty. I wiped tears away, one stream at a time, hoping that God would take his tears and add them to the millions that I'd seen before. I had no remorse; I felt nothing. I wanted to feel guilty for not understanding him but when the tables were turned, he felt no guilt for me. I was in the state of betrayal and the strange thing is, I continue playing this role. How many times must my heart suffer before I realize that people are selfish and only care about themselves at the end of the day?

As I continue to turn the other cheek, hatred for him builds up inside like plaque around my heart. I don't hate him but I despise everything that is deceitful in his character. I put him on a pedestal and now I sit back and watch it fall apart as I pick up the crumbled pieces of his imaginary throne.

Letting Go of the One I Love

I am in love. I almost detest what I feel especially when it isn't reciprocated by the individual I adore. I find myself drifting away, consumed in my thoughts of him. Boggling questions like how and when did I get so caught up into someone who clearly isn't ready for what I have to offer plague me. I ended it with him like I had others in the past. Except somehow, this time, it's real. I grew a brain and substantial standards. Why did it take the unthinkable for me to do such a thing?

My lying lips say it's over but, with every painful beat, my open heart keeps confessing the truth: "I love him; I am in love with him". My lips uttered callous but honest words that cut him like a knife. These words that shone light on how my heart really ached from his actions, caused him to run and hide. The shame and embarrassment of it all overwhelmed him, so he faded to black, laid low and waddled in self pity.

I could have been kinder in my delivery but I was so full of negative emotions, I simply could not contain myself. I was wondering who he thought he was. He should be grateful to even be in my presence, the presence of a queen. Yet, no matter how hard I try, he still doesn't see me for who I am. The harder I try the more he resists. This relationship was a no win situation; we were doomed from the start. I had to learn the hard way and what suffered was my heart.

He took my kindness for weakness and now my outlook on men is all twisted and distorted. Will I ever learn to love again without fear of being hurt? Who knows? I know that I love him but until he is ready I will let him go. His essence though will continue to be etched on my heart, embracing my soul for what is to come.

What's In Store For Me?

I have so much hurt and pain in my heart. It feels like salt being poured into an open wound. I pray that I could be emotionless. What would the world be like without feelings? I want that, I want to be numb. I want my feelings to be sedated and maybe, just maybe, I can see things differently. Life wouldn't be so complicated. These tears would stop flowing like a drippy faucet.

I pray for peace to comfort me. I want to be happy, filled with the colors of warmth like Joseph's coat of many colors. You can buy many things but happiness isn't one of them. I have had thoughts of death but was quickly swayed by the laughter of my children; they saved me. The innocent ones, my pride and joy, they bring me salvation. Happiness is what I want to find.

It's like a needle in a hay stack waiting for me, calling my name. All I have to do is answer the call, but I am afraid, afraid to taste and see what life holds for me.

Overlooking the Obvious

Have I been overlooking the obvious? Why is that when men say they don't want a relationship, women take it as a challenge, hoping to change their minds? How would anyone benefit from this ongoing battle? Maybe if I buy him whatever his heart desires, I could win him over. He just doesn't know what he wants right now but I will guide him to the light. I know: I will give him my body, fulfill his every fantasy as often as he wishes then I will have him; I'm just sure of it.

Better yet, I will make myself so available that he wouldn't have a choice but to fall in love with me. I will cook all of his favorite dishes since the way to a man's heart is through his stomach. I will make sure that I keep my appearance up just for him; I don't want any other women diverting his attention away from me. So I ask him again, where do you see our relationship going? He replies nonchalantly "I told you in the beginning, I am not ready for a relationship. I am not saying that we will never be together but just not right now."

Words cannot express the way these same words continue to shatter my heart into a million pieces. My face is expressionless but behind the mask it is broken beyond repair. I silently question whether I am simply not good enough? I think of how, even though he said those words time and time again, his actions showed something altogether different.

Do I surrender to defeat? Of course not. He just doesn't know that we are destined to be together. I live and breathe him and it's apparent that he does too since his actions say so. I find myself regrouping in order to unleash plan "B". I will buy him whatever he wants since money isn't an object anymore, especially when it comes to love. I was so happy to surprise him with his dream car: fully loaded, leather interior, custom made rims.

In my mind, the gesture was priceless, even though it set me back a few pennies. Who cares that I am still sporting a lemon? I just want to make him happy because I love him. I did notice a change in his behavior; he called me more often. Even though I received a cut off notice for my utilities, I was glad to know that he was happy. So I asked the dreaded question again and got the same response. I am left looking like a fool once again but its okay because I have a better plan this time.

When that plan failed I sat back and asked myself if I was clinically insane. I continue to do the same thing over and over and expect a different outcome, only to be utterly ashamed because the result is the same. Yes, I had lost my mind and my identity. The battle overcame me. I finally decided to walk away. I realized that winning his love and affection wasn't worth all of the time and effort. My heart is no longer on the auction block; he wasn't worthy of me and never will be.

When the Smoke Cleared

When the smoke cleared I made the right decision to let you go. I realized that you were not good for me but I did enjoy you for the moment. I must admit that there is a part of me that desires to know if you would have changed your mind and chose me. Nothing about our relationship was healthy but I lived and learned. When we had our good times they were good. But when we had bad times, they were just that "bad." Being caught in your web was mentally draining. My natural effervescence began to seep away and it was replaced with pain and heartache.

The stench of deceit lingered when I discovered that you were not truly what I perceived you to be. Love blinded me, love made a fool of me; love altered my ability to see through the mind games that you continued to play. Subsequently, I question why it is exceptionally hard for me to find it in my tattered heart to forgive you. Rage infuriates my soul, knowing the secret you kept hidden so meticulously, and how you continued to deny the fact that you had common knowledge all the while.

When all is said and done I still feel that even a person so cunning, hiding behind the mask of doubt and deception can be loved. When you see me know that the beauty you see is only what God allows you to see as I am still under repair from the toll you took on my inner being. I trust God to deal with you, make you shiny and brand new. Your road will not be easy but in the end what I saw in you will come to pass and you will be what He desires for you to be.

Rejection

Rejection has embedded itself in my heart. It feels like a raging sea that cannot be calmed. It destroys everything in its path and leaves no survivors. I have been rejected too often, not by strangers, but by the very people that I care for most. When I look at other people and their relationships, I wonder what I'm doing wrong.

My heart beats in agony each time I try to reach out for an ounce of acceptance only to be cast away to the wolves that take delight in slowly devouring me. There aren't words to express how my wretched heart continues to be massacred by rejection. Rejection does not discriminate. It is so a part of my life. I have embraced its solace. As much as I hate the pain, I revel in its black hole of deceit. I am rejection's prisoner. I lie awake at night in misery as rejection obliterates my soul. The throbbing pain causes me to cry out in despair. I pray for someone, anyone to hear my desperate cry.

    I just want to be loved but the love that I so desire is beyond my reach. It's unattainable. There are no vacancies here since rejection set up residence in my soul. Rejection is an all too familiar place that will never go away. It saturates my very being. Desolate and alone, I find myself praying for solitude. This is my way of life and rejection is a part of my very essence, until the end of time.

Living a Lie

All the heartbreak of my marriage keeps me asking the question, who pays for my ex's mistakes? I never imagined that this would happen to me. I gave him everything, my all and this is the thanks that I get. At times, I wished I were invisible. I rushed home to cater to my husband the way the Bible taught me. I know marriage ain't all roses but I was willing to make it work.

He was my knight and shining armor; nothing could make me see him any differently. He was the love of my life. I showed him things that no other woman would take the time out to show. I opened up to him and shared my most intimate secrets, only to be betrayed. I didn't deserve that; I didn't deserve to be made to feel like less of a woman. But there I was, pathetic and all.

When he stayed out late at night, it didn't bother me; just as long as he came home – that was the song I sang time and time again. When he was too high to even pay attention to his children, I thought - this will pass. When the phone rang all hours of the night, I laughed and thought, she doesn't have as much of a hold as she thought because he didn't answer her calls. I wasn't stupid; I knew he had other women. But as long as he came home to me, who cared?

How much more of this would I be expected to take: the excuses, the partying and the staying out all night? The excuses he fed me about why he never had any money were never true because the truth was, he gave it to the others. Whatever happened to home is where the heart is? This was not the case in my situation. The uncontrollable crying at night was unbearable. The mental anguish that I put myself through was excruciating. The fact that I would never be good enough for him no matter what efforts I put forth to win his heart was pitiful. This was my marriage. It's called living a lie.

Woman Scorned

Was I crazy for calling up your mistress to let her know that we were still together? I don't think so! I mean, even though we were separated at the time, it wasn't right for you to move on and create another instant family. Oh, so you're playing daddy now? What about our children? You know, the children that I endured hard labor for, just to see the satisfaction in your eyes. Do you remember them or ole' girl got you so caught up that they are just a figment of your imagination?

Yep, I got her shaking in her boots because she realizes that she is messing with the right one. I wonder if she's lost in thought about how I know where she lives, how much her house is worth or the fact that I know where she works and her salary base as well. I can't help but sit back and laugh at the fact that I am so much smarter than both of you.

Hell, I could have bought her with a wooden nickel when I told her to get ready to play momma since that is what you are looking for. It's not all her fault though. I can't blame her because you are just as much a fool as she is. You could have waited until the divorce was final before you decided to move on. Better yet, remove my name from your property. You strut around, calling yourself a man; coward suits you better.

I wondered when you were going to figure out that I was the one who told the repo man where to find your vehicle. How does it feel to be walking now? I bet you are in great shape! I am not crazy; I just want you to know that you created a monster; a monster named 'woman scorned'. Did you get your child support papers yet? Merry Christmas from the kids and me. We hope you really enjoy it because my attorney and I went to great lengths searching for the perfect gift for you this year.

While I am not crazy, I am a firm believer in karma.

I was just as surprised as you when I pulled your call log to see that you were calling your mistress all times of the night. Was she the one you bought the dozen roses and lavish gifts for? This is what I found when I browsed through you credit card bills because it sure as hell wasn't me you were shopping for. All the extensive business trips that caused you to be away weeks at a time, is this where the 18 year old bill was incurred?

Man you really did a number on me but its okay because that alimony settlement will really come in handy. I wish you and your mistress the best. Last, but certainly not least, tell her I said thank you for lifting my burdens. Now maybe she can be a big girl and put some of your bills in her name too.

Emotionally Bankrupt

Emotionally bankrupt is how many feel when it comes to love. Love has so many rules and guidelines. Many seek love in order to fill the vacancy in their heart. In this day and time, it's not unusual to be uncomfortable in your own skin, especially when you know that something is missing. Have you ever put all of your love on the line only to have it snatched away, leaving you feeling stripped and naked? Who do you file a report with when someone has literally stolen your heart only to return it all battered and bruised?

You find yourself wondering if the damage can be undone. The desire to be isolated and alone is a recipe for a great depression as it lingers in the hearts of many. Withdrawal after withdrawal is made. Waiting on a deposit that equals or exceeds the love you've given causes your heart to be overdrawn. Can a broken heart accrue interest?

Was love created to feel like a form of capital punishment? These are the questions that linger in my heart. This is how I feel after love has come and gone.

Cursed

Why did I put him on a pedestal? I thought he was everything that a man could be in life. I looked past the obvious, hoping that certain characteristics would fade. Love blinded me but only so much. The rest I blame on just wanting to be accepted by him. I was glad just to get a fraction of his time even though it appeared to mean nothing to him. It was apparent that he wasn't as interested as I was but I thought with time, he would get there; he just needed some coaxing.

I enjoyed his brilliance; his thought process amazed me so. He was not my knight in shining armor though. He was a deceiver dressed up in lies. I was his puppet; I danced, being strung along by his words. He was like poison infecting my soul making me hollow inside and out. When he left, I thought I would die. But in his absence, I realized that indeed, he left me with a curse.

I want to be pure and innocent again. I want to be free from this bondage. He left me tainted and broken beyond repair. When my true prince finally comes along, will he be able to accept me or will he resent me for being used goods? These thoughts haunt me; I am tormented because the man that I thought truly loved and adored me kept a fatal secret, a curse that will haunt me until the end of time.

Without You

Can't explain how I feel; it's difficult to put into words - the emotions that seem to conquer me. Colors illuminate and shine bright to overcome darkness. I try not to be blue but when I look into yours eyes I see guilt and torment. I am so uncertain of your actions. You have yet to clarify where you stand. Do you really love or just pretend? I want so badly for us to be friends but the hurt lingers. Could it be possible that you have truly changed?

I listen carefully to the words fall so smoothly from your lips. As I take specimen to my lab of thoughts, I dissect them carefully, looking with the microscopic veins of my heart trying to determine what this cell of bondage can be classified as. The results produce something unknown. Here I am, back at square one, suffering from the effects of you haunting me.

Why do I entertain you? Nothing you say has made me feel secure enough to trust you. I envisioned us being one, in love for all time. All of that was make-believe though. You made it possible for me to see that love is a fairy tale, lifeless words mapped out on sheets of paper with only the ability to take flight in our minds. All things have an ending; I find this statement to be true. I thought I was lost until I came to grips with the fact that I am a better person without you.

Love Detox

If only you knew my inner thoughts, then you would truly understand my resistance. The naked truth is that love is nothing like the half of what I expected it would be. I thought love would be something oh so magical and melodic to my soul. Instead, it blinded me and caused nothing but pain and despair. I tried love once again in hopes that it would change my mindset; but again, love put a bitter taste in my mouth.

I sat and wondered why I desired love so. Love was apart of me, but when I thought I found the one I'd share my love with, I was left desolate and alone. If I could describe the taste of love, it would be bittersweet. I tasted love's nectar but it pulled me deeper and deeper into its tangled web. Once I reached love's core, the taste of venom embraced me then penetrated my soul. I frantically tried to endure love's fatal sting, hoping that God would have mercy on me and send the cure.

 I wait ever so patiently, still believing that love is not so bad. I continuously believe that there is hope for me. Love has betrayed me but I remain faithful, hoping that love will one day desire and engulf me without leaving another brutal scar. I will barricade my feelings and desires until love allows me to feel safe again.

Now You Want Me

I's strange that you called me out of the blue, interested in me again, now that you know I have someone new. Only a question mark forms as I wonder what more you could possibly want from me, especially since you already had my head. You try to pick up like nothing ever happened, like you never hurt me to my core. When I hear your voice, this sudden pain hits me, rocking an otherwise calm boat at the shore of life's sea.

I thought that I ended things appropriately, after writing you a four-paged letter that expressed how I felt. I thought maybe you would be melancholy but instead your arrogance dwelt, lingering like the stench of week old garbage infested with maggots. The very thought of it made me cringe. I hoped that leaving you alone would make you humble yourself and realize that you're not the only fish in the sea. Instead, what I have before me is a monster that I created, a nigga with a big head and whorish tendencies.

As I listen to you carry on and on about how you've changed, I feel sick to my stomach because something about you just ain't right. I can't really take you seriously; when I did, you had me fooled - blinded by lies and pipe dreams. That is all that held you together, bonded with super glue. I hope you're not seriously thinking you can weasel your way back into my life. Dealing with you made me feel like I sold my soul to the devil and my heart was the ultimate sacrifice.

You keep reiterating how you have seen the light, that your actions were selfish. You keep saying over and over again "baby I didn't mean to hurt you". It's obvious that regret has taken over your life but your apologies are not welcome here. Sorry boo! I have shut the door on my past and I hate to inform you that you are a part of it. So take my advice and move on; consider it a lesson learned at last.

Chapter Eight:

My Truth-Seeking Heart

Brainstorming

I have learned that accepting people at face value is a hard task to accomplish. God loves me faithfully. No matter how many times I mess up, He is always there to guide me and put me back on track. Now, if He can do this for me, why can't I seem to do this for others? God has a way of revealing people, exposing their true intentions, whether good or bad. A wise woman once told me, if you listen close enough, a person will tell you what's truly in their heart if you just take the cotton out of your ears and place it in your mouth.

I began to think about God's word. He says that if anyone says, I *love* God, and hates his brother, he is a liar; for he who does not *love* his brother whom he has seen cannot *love* God whom he has not seen. It can't be any plainer than this. I sit and wonder why I deal with issues that cause me to look deeper into my heart. When I look, the only thing I find is a mirror, reflecting an image of me. I have been forced to put myself in the other person's shoes, only to realize that I can't hate the person, only their actions.

Take me as I am - this is what I see when I look deep into the eyes of the beholder. I respond by saying, I love you, flaws and all; meaning I love you even when you do wrong. I sit back and ponder why people still feel ashamed and embarrassed by their actions when clearly all is forgiven. Is it that one has been exposed and you can see him or her for who they really are? I guess I will never fully understand the reasoning behind all the madness, but I do know that I am a woman after God's own heart and when you see me, it is Him you see.

A New Day

This is a new day and it's all about me!! If I had a chance to change the past I would gladly decline. If it wasn't for my past, I wouldn't be where I am today. This is a new day; I am walking away from the past hurt and pain. Why sit and wallow in self pity when there is so much to live for? Life is a beautiful thing. It teaches life-long lessons: not to become but to push on.

It's a new day!! A new day for love, love for me, love for life, a love to know what is destined for me. This is a new start: loving myself, accepting myself. Being aware of the fact that I am who I am and nothing can change that. Hey, it's a new day. My life will be like spring blooming into what I am supposed to be, because I have a purpose. I have a purpose to stand tall, be strong and walk into my destiny.

It is definitely a new day for so many possibilities.

When I take a breath, I feel as if I am that sparrow Marvin heard singing. I feel so much strength, so much power. It's a new day and I thank God for allowing me to see that it's okay to reinvent me.

Torn With What's Destined

I continue to wonder if I am missing out on a good life. How is it that I can be so utterly foolish? There is someone who dwells in my safe place but I'm not quite ready for what is being offered. Then there is the new life that has been laid before me. I though, am too afraid to see what's behind door number two, afraid of being hurt. It looks so promising but I sense that it probably isn't all that it seems to be. Door number two claims to offer happiness, wealth and experiences beyond anything that I have imagined. At what cost? Must I give my all only to discover betrayal once again? My poor heart cannot take another horrendous blow.

When I decide to take that chance and move in the direction of the seemingly blissful life that door number two offers, I become uneasy; I sense something unexplainable in my spirit. I try to shake it off, labeling my fear as fretfulness of completion. But it is still something there in the mist. I take baby steps as I come closer to door number two, when I hear in the distance a familiar voice that causes me to stop dead in my tracks. How I yearn to run to my comfort zone but I have traveled such a distance, I can no longer see him. His voice beckons for me not to leave him. As my eyes begin to well up with the tears that I thought were buried so deep inside, I turn to see his face once again before walking into my intended purpose-filled life.

From where I stood, it seemed like miles of inaccessibility. I could still hear my comfort zone crying out, not wanting me to let go, wanting me to not forget what we had. He was trying to remind me of our past, of how good it was and how great it could be if I would just be patient. I began to reminisce on the good and bad times my comfort zone and I shared. I just couldn't let go of the endless frustration, humiliation and agony my comfort zone caused me. All I ever wanted was for him to just see and accept me for who I was. I recalled being ever so patient, entertaining him and his little antics. I always said I should leave my comfort zone, but I was unable to detach. While pondering these things, I began to walk closer to door number two, even though I still felt unsure about it. It really was worth taking a chance on. Door number two was beautiful, elegantly detailed and made. It was an exquisite site; I tried to take it all in at once but I had to keep looking again and again to make sure it was real. When I accepted door number two's offer I felt so much peace. I thought I would never feel serenity like this. Happiness finally came after what seemed like an eternity of waiting. I don't want to let this moment go. I accepted the offer and I promised myself that I would never look back. I consider everything else that occurred in my life as a lesson learned. I am taking this opportunity and allowing myself to be happy and whatever happens will be worth taking a chance.

Guarded

I lay here listening to the stillness of the night, wondering if you think of me as often as I think of you. If there were any way possible that I could be by your side, I would make it happen. But it's best that we are apart. When I am near you I can hardly contain myself. I fall victim to the urgency of longing to just be in your arms. I want to be the one for you, the one who cares for you and the one who takes out the time to listen to you when you need reassuring. But being near you is like kryptonite blinding my judgment.

I have been down this road of regret before, along with vowing not to dwell in its path again. Love has a tendency to always find me at the crossroads. No matter how hard I try to fight it, love trickles into my guarded heart. I love hard, allowing my feelings to be visible to the naked eye, only to be crushed and misused. Maybe I pick the wrong people, people who are undeserving of my love.

Maybe this is how love goes until the right one finds me.

Yet, I can't stop my mind from thinking of you.

Searching

I wanna step out of the box but what drives me is so obvious, it makes me keep asking for more. I try to hide it but my tell/tale heart seemingly gives me away. The drumming of my tell/tale heart thumps so loudly, I sense that everyone takes notice of the piercing beat. Prisoner of my own thoughts; caught up in my fantasy world, believing that everyone still has some good left in them. Why must it be this way? I try to assess my status, evaluate why my kind heart continues to engage in things that are not healthy for it.

My free spiritedness has no limits. I search my heart for the answers, but it had nothing left to say. Am I that blinded by the fear of being alone that I disregard my own intuitions? I stand alone, frustrated and hurt, seeking an easy way out of my mess, hoping that the next lesson won't be so hard to learn. Everything that I have encountered in my life continues to be a process of self-inflicted pain, derived from neediness. Preconceived notions are on my mind but when I attempt to act them out it only turns into more drama.

 I'm my own worse enemy. I am still driven, searching for something new, something different to fill this void in my life. I continue to turn to love to be my healer, even though it seems that love may not be on my side. There is no trouble-free method for my circumstances. When I examined it for what it was, I found that the real issue was me. I find myself searching, searching.

Issues

I hate being alone. The very thought makes me sick to my stomach. Having to deal with my own thoughts and the hash things I've learned about myself is unnerving. Not wanting to face reality and all of the many issues that it entails is my way of life. Why I choose the routes that I do is beyond my understanding. Being unsure of myself, saying one thing and doing the total opposite is normal. My moods can be tricky at times, depending on the day. I allow people to get close to me only to push them away.

Lonely in a room filled with people is a familiar scene for me. I sit back and observe everyone delighting in each other while I marinate in my season of loneliness. I wear my mask well in this masquerade party called life. I hide behind my fears, praying that I don't break. Walking tall. Dressed to impress. Putting up a front that I have managed for so long. Is it hard being me? Damn right it is.

It's frustrating to have people look to me for strength and guidance when I can barely help myself.

You're probably saying wow, she has some issues.

I totally agree. Show me someone who doesn't and I will show you someone who desires to be set free. My soul will not rest. It is caught up at purgatory's crossroad, waiting for a divine intervention that will bring inner peace. Things are not always what they seem. People are not always how they portray themselves to be. I have learned that many people have issues and that includes me.

Change

Has it finally come to this? The time to allow change in my life: some major, some minor, some great, some miniscule. I need to do this and not just say I'm doing it because it needs to be done. I have allowed my precious time to be wasted in circumstances that didn't require my presence. Not able to let go, afraid of the outcome, vulnerable to the affects of its disillusion.   To give up something that I desire completely is devastating. A sign of growth is learning that wanting and needing are two different arts.

Giving up is so very hard to do but I am running a race that cannot be won. It took some time for me to see this and it took even longer for me to believe it. I can only give so much of me, only to receive half or nothing at all. Isn't it amazing how one thing leads to another, like a chain reaction? Never really dealing with the root of the problem can be even more damaging. Peace of mind is what I am striving for. Drama free is what I desire to be. Dragging along baggage will not help, it will only hinder me.

Despite the what if's and maybe's that were causing my hope factor to slowly deteriorate, believing that one day things would change was absurd. I have decided to take the next step and change, since others were too afraid to follow the yellow brick road, too afraid to gain the courage in order to do so. In the end no one wants to be the bad guy. They would rather throw the stone and hide their hand. I can't deny that I'm tired of disappointing myself and making my Savior cry.

Peace of Mind

Peace of mind is very hard to come by and believe me I speak from experience. I can truly say there is nothing like it and nothing that can compare to this serene experience. Peace of mind is priceless; it can't be bought. I have always desired to be rich but even millionaires encounter problems. I heard that the more [money] you have the more problems you inherit.

I still struggle with the situations of life. I have encountered so much peace. No matter what comes my way, I just think of people who have stumbled upon circumstances that render them helpless and who are in a worse state than me. I embrace peace as if it were my knight in shining armor. Don't get me wrong, I am still human and have human reactions. However, there is only one thing that matters in my life and that is peace of mind.

𝒫eace of mind has crowned me and I have become heir to the throne of tranquility. My rights of passage consist of a mindset that calls for God to grant me the serenity to accept the things I cannot change, the courage to change the things I can and the wisdom to know the difference. I have allowed peace to overtake me. I have surrendered all of my anxieties, worries and fears which in the end are trivial.

ℐ longed for peace of mind. It was an insatiable craving like known other. It was like an unquenchable thirst. Once I realized that peace of mind was free to anyone who yearned for it, I seized the moment and never let go. So if you see me now and wonder what's so different, it's called Peace of Mind: my rescuer, my liberator, my redeemer, my all and all.

Silence

Silence is a language that most people don't understand. The absence of speech has confused many, especially those who fail to understand that sometimes it's best to just remain silent to avoid crucifying another's feelings. Silence is not always easy. In fact, those who have mastered this phenomenon are carefree and seemingly at peace. I was asked if I had the option of having a super human power which would I choose.

I pondered this question, if I had the ability to read minds, it would probably cause more trouble than its worth. Being invisible would certainly ruin the suspense, especially since some things are best left to the imagination. Even though it wasn't on the list of super human powers or abilities, I chose silence.

You see, mastering the art of silence is on the same level as letting go and allowing God to handle your circumstances. Silence is also on the same level as mastering being alone, having an intimate relationship with God, and being okay with self. Silence can be interpreted in a lot of ways but at the end of the day it is eloquent yet misunderstood. I was taught that embracing silence takes courage. A wise person realizes that there is a time and place for everything, a time to keep silent and a time to speak.

Please don't get me wrong, I am human and have thoughts like anyone else. But no matter how intense things become, no matter how people may set out to hurt or destroy me, silence is always the key. One can only read so much into no response at all. At first, the idea of silence was cloudy; but the picture has become clearer to me. It's okay to just be still. Everything doesn't deserve a reaction.

At this time, at this moment and in this place I am ok with being patient. I am consumed in quietness, secure in trusting God, prospering in the ability to just be strong, embellishing in calmness and taking silence by the hand. Silence is a state of mind that if sought, will yield peace with rewards of faith. Only believe.

Made in the USA
Charleston, SC
27 February 2011